Character Education

Tolerance

by Lucia Raatma

Consultant:
Madonna Murphy, Ph.D.
Associate Professor of Education
University of St. Francis, Joliet, Illinois
Author, *Character Education in America's
Blue Ribbon Schools*

Bridgestone Books
an imprint of Capstone Press
Mankato, Minnesota

Bridgestone Books are published by Capstone Press
818 North Willow Street, Mankato, Minnesota 56001
http://www.capstone-press.com

Library of Congress Cataloging-in-Publication Data
Raatma, Lucia.
   Tolerance/by Lucia Raatma.
   p. cm.—(Character education)
   Includes bibliographical references (p.24) and index.
   Summary: Describes tolerance as a virtue and suggests ways in which it can
be recognized and practiced.
   ISBN 0-7368-0373-4
   1. Toleration—Juvenile literature. [1. Toleration.] I. Title. II. Series.
BJ1431.R23 2000
179′.9—dc21   99-29180
                                                                              CIP

Editorial Credits
Damian Koshnick, editor; Heather Kindseth, cover designer and illustrator;
   Kimberly Danger photo researcher

Photo Credits
GeoIMAGERY/Jan Wilson Jorolan, 10
Gregg R. Andersen, cover
Photo Network/Myrleen Ferguson Cate, 16
Photri-Microstock/FOTOPIC, 4; MacDonald Photography, 6
Telegraph Color Library, 8; FPG, 18/FPG International LLC
Unicorn Stock Photography/Joel Dexter, 14
Uniphoto, 20
Visuals Unlimited/Jeff Greenberg, 12

Table of Contents

Tolerance

Tolerance is about accepting the differences between people. It is learning to enjoy the differences you see in others. Being tolerant means understanding that people often are different from what you expect.

accept

to take things and people as they are

Tolerance with Yourself

People make mistakes. For example, you may forget to do your homework. You might feel bad when your teacher asks for your homework. Tolerant people accept that they sometimes make mistakes. Tolerant people know that they can learn from their mistakes.

Tolerance with Your Family

You may not always agree with your family. Your older sister may not like meat. But you might enjoy hamburgers. Your dad may like tennis. But you may prefer soccer. Tolerant people appreciate that each person in their family is different.

appreciate

to enjoy or value something or someone

Tolerance with Your Friends

Being tolerant means allowing others
to have their own likes and dislikes.
You might like to watch the monkeys
at the zoo. Your friend might like to
see the elephants. A tolerant person
would not complain about seeing
the elephants.

Tolerance in Sports

Playing team sports can be fun. But your team might not always play well. Someone might strike out in a baseball game. Or your team may lose a game. Tolerant people do not get angry when they lose. They have fun playing whether they win or lose.

Tolerance at School

Tolerant people are willing to learn new things. You might meet a new friend during recess. Your friend might want to play a game you do not know. The game may be hard to understand at first. But it might be fun if you are willing to learn.

Tolerance in the Community

All people look and act differently.
People have different skin colors. They
wear different clothes and speak many
languages. Tolerant people do not
judge others by how they look.
Tolerant people know that these
differences do not matter.

"Whenever I see an erring man, I say to myself I have also erred; . . .and in this way I feel kinship with everyone in the world . . ."
–Mahatma Gandhi

Tolerance and Mahatma Gandhi

Mahatma Gandhi was born in India in 1869. He taught people that violence does not solve problems. Gandhi worked peacefully with others to solve problems. He talked and listened even when he did not agree with others. Gandhi was a tolerant person.

violence

the use of physical force

Learning from Tolerance

Tolerant people are willing to listen to new ideas. They often learn something from other people's ideas. Being tolerant does not mean you have to agree with everyone. It only means that you are willing to listen. Listening is an important part of learning.

Hands On: Make a Puzzle

Learn about your friends by making a puzzle together.

What You Need

A marker
A large piece of paper
A group of three or more friends

What You Do

1. Draw a puzzle on the piece of paper.
2. Make a puzzle piece for each person in the group.
3. Cut out the pieces.
4. Have everyone take a puzzle piece.
5. Have your friends write something that they like or dislike on their puzzle pieces.
6. Put the puzzle back together piece by piece.
7. Each piece of the puzzle represents a person.

Ask your friends about what they wrote on their puzzle pieces. Tell them about what you wrote on your puzzle piece. Part of tolerance is understanding and accepting people's likes and dislikes.

Words to Know

belief (bi-LEEF)—something thought of as true or correct

complain (kuhm-PLAYN)—to say that you are unhappy about something

err (AHR)—to do wrong; to make a mistake.

idea (eye-DEE-uh)—a thought, a plan, or an opinion

judge (JUHJ)—to form a belief about something or someone

solve (SOLV)—to find the answer to a problem

violence (VYE-uh-luhnss)—the use of physical force; violence often hurts other people.

Read More

Fisher, Leonard Everett. *Gandhi.* New York: Atheneum Books for Young Readers, 1995.

Manning, Brennan. *The Boy Who Cried Abba: A Parable of Trust and Acceptance.* San Francisco: Harper San Francisco, 1997.

Williams, Mary Lowe. *Let's Celebrate Our Differences.* Deerfield Beach, Fla.: Health Communications, 1994.

Internet Sites

Adventures from the Book of Virtues Home Page
http://www.pbs.org/adventures
Character Counts Carousel
http://www.charactercounts.org/carousel.htm
The People for Peace Conflict Resolution Center
http://members.aol.com/pforpeace/WorkItOut

Index